CHECK YOUR ENGLISH VOCABULARY FOR

COMPUTERS

AND

INFORMATION TECHNOLOGY

Jon Marks

BLOOMSBURY

First edition published 1995
Second edition published 1999

Third edition published in Great Britain 2007 by
A&CBlack Publishers Ltd

Reprinted 2012
Bloomsbury Publishing Plc
50 Bedford Square
London WC1B 3DP

A CIP entry for this book is available from the British Library.
ISBN-13: 978 0 7136 7917 5

This book is produced using paper that is made from wood grown in managed, sustainable forests.
It is natural, renewable and recyclable. The logging and manufacturing processes conform to the
environmental regulations of the country of origin.

Text typeset by A & C Black
Printed in India by Replika Press

Contents

Introduction

Who is the book for?

This book has been written for people whose first language is not English, and who use or are going to use computers and other information technology in an English-speaking environment. It covers the language needed to use information technology equipment, work with computer programs, discuss problems and plan projects. It does not cover advanced technical vocabulary for computer programmers or electronic engineers. All the language in the book is intended to be accessible to intermediate level students and above.

How can the book be used?

The vocabulary is arranged by topic. Choose the topics that interest you. The pages do not have to be completed in any particular order, and there is no need to complete all the pages if some are on topics which are not useful to you. It is better to complete one or two pages in a day, and remember the vocabulary, rather than completing as many pages as possible. The answers to the exercises can be found at the back of the book. There is also an index to help you find the pages which are most useful to you.

Write new words and phrases you learn in a notebook or file. Review this language regularly so that it becomes part of your active vocabulary.

A good general dictionary will be very helpful, providing pronunciation guides and more contexts. For vocabulary relating specifically to computers, *Dictionary of Computing* (A&C Black, ISBN 978 07475 6622 9) will be a useful reference source.

Section 1: Hardware

1.1 Hardware

1. battery
2. cable
3. desktop computer
4. digital camera
5. docking station
6. fax machine
7. laptop computer (or notebook)
8. mobile phone
9. mouse
10. PDA (Personal Digital Assistant)
11. plug
12. printer
13. projector
14. scanner
15. socket

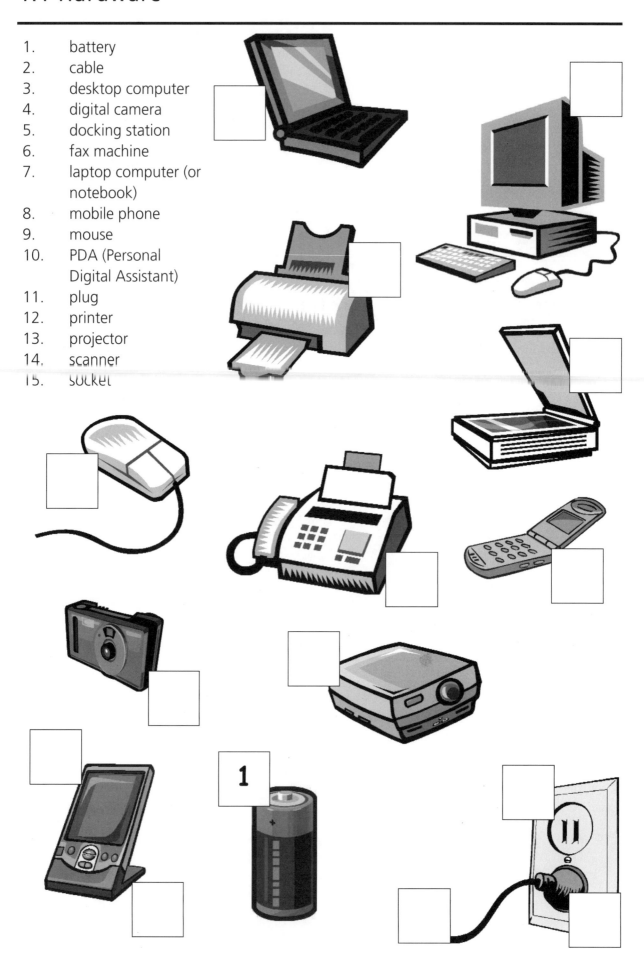

For reference see A & C Black *Dictionary of Computing* (978 07475 6622 9).

A. Match the verbs with the nouns.

1.	recharge	a.	digital photos
2.	click on	b.	faxes
3.	dial	c.	a number on your mobile phone
4.	give	d.	a presentation
5.	move	e.	something with the mouse
6.	print out	f.	the battery
7.	send and receive	g.	the mouse
8.	take some	h.	twenty pages

B. Choose the best verb.

9. To turn on the computer, _____ the "Start" button.

   a. touch   **b.** press   **c.** switch

10. The printer has _____ of ink.

   a. finished   **b.** ended   **c.** run out

11. Unfortunately, my scanner isn't _____ at the moment.

   a. working   **b.** going   **c.** doing

12. Please _____ the CD ROM.

   a. insert   **b.** introduce   **c.** inject

13. The projector isn't working because it isn't _____.

   a. plugged   **b.** plugged in   **c.** plugged into

14. The batteries in my digital camera are nearly dead. They need _____.

   a. to change   **b.** exchanging   **c.** changing

15. I have to _____ a computer screen for eight hours a day.

   a. see   **b.** look at   **c.** watch

16. Switch off your computer, and _____ it from the wall socket.

   a. de-plug   **b.** unplug   **c.** non-plug

17. I turned off the photocopier and _____ the plug.

   a. pulled out   **b.** extracted   **c.** took away

18. _____ any key to continue.

   a. Kick   **b.** Smash   **c.** Hit

7

1.3 The workstation

CD drive / DVD drive
CRT monitor
flat panel monitor
floppy disk drive
key
keyboard
mouse
power button
screen
stand
tower
wire / cable

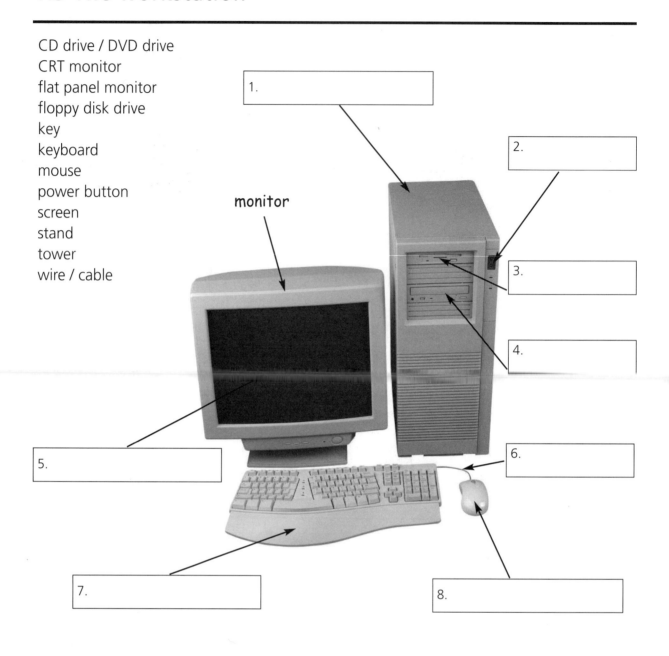

1.

2.

monitor

3.

4.

5.

6.

7.

8.

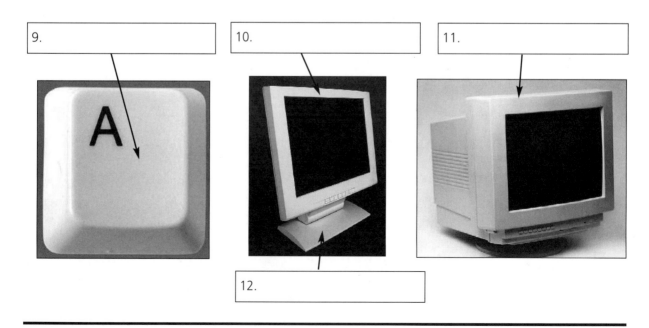

9.

10.

11.

12.

For reference see A & C Black *Dictionary of Computing* (978 07475 6622 9).

Rearrange the letters to make things which can be part of a workstation.

tucmepor	computer
13. trirpen	_____
14. nasecnr	_____
15. kesd	_____
16. hacir	_____
17. nopelethe	_____

Choose the best word.

18. The mouse moves on a _____.

    a. mouse mat   **b.** mouse carpet   **c.** mouse table

19. TV and computer screens are usually measured in _____.

    a. feet   **b.** miles   **c.** inches

20. Before you start work, _____ the height of your chair

    a. adjust   **b.** change   **c.** rearrange

21. To get sound from your computer, plug in a pair of _____.

    a. loudhailers   **b.** loudspeakers   **c.** loud voices

22. The computer is connected to the telephone line via a _____.

    a. module   **b.** modem   **c.** mod

23. You can increase the functions or performance of a computer with an _____.

    a. extension card   **b.** exploding card   **c.** expansion card

24. Mobile phones and PDAs can communicate with computers via _____.

    a. Bluebeard ®   **b.** Blueberry ®   **c.** Bluetooth ®

25. There's a spare _____ in the workstation…

    a. electric hole   **b.** power point   **c.** electrical opening

26. …so you can plug in your mobile phone _____.

    a. charger   **b.** power   **c.** electrification

27. SD cards can be read in a computer's _____.

    a. storage reader   **b.** memory reader   **c.** card reader

For reference see A & C Black *Dictionary of Computing* (978 07475 6622 9).

1.4 The keyboard

space bar   alphabet keys   calculator keys

function keys   return key (or enter key)   indicator lights

shift key   alt key   control key   escape key

delete key   tab key   caps lock key   backspace key

1. To go back one space, hit the _____.
2. To change to capital letters, press the _____.
3. To change the capital letters permanently, hit the _____.
4. To insert a tabulation, press the _____.
5. To activate the "Ctrl" functions, press the _____.
6. To activate the "alt" functions, hit the _____.
7. To stop the computer doing something, you can press the

_____.

8. Select the text you want to remove, and hit the _____.

> **You can say "key" or "button"**

standard keyboard   ergonomic keyboard

key in (or type in)   enter   data input

9.   Please _____ your password.
10.   It took me two hours to _____ all that text.
11.   A keyboard is a _____ device.
12.   Do you have a _____?
     No. I have a special _____. It's better for my arms and back.

For reference see A & C Black *Dictionary of Computing* (978 07475 6622 9).

pointer	on	optical	roll
scroll up	scroll down	touchpad	left button
right button	joystick	single	double
scroll wheel	hold down	repetitive strain injury	

1. _____ to see pages above.

2. _____ to see pages below.

3. To select text, _____ the left button, and move the mouse pointer.

4. If you use a mouse for many hours every day, you can get _____ in your fingers.

5. With a laptop computer, plug in a mouse, or use the _____ in front of the keyboard.

6. To play some games, you need to use a _____ instead of a mouse.

7. To move up and down a page, you can _____ the mouse wheel.

8. This mouse doesn't have a ball. It's an _____ mouse.

9. One click of a mouse button is called a _____ click.

10. Two clicks of a mouse button are called a _____ click.

11. Click _____ the folder to open it.

12. _____

13. _____

14. _____

15. _____

A wheel mouse

For reference see A & C Black *Dictionary of Computing* (978 07475 6622 9).

1.6 Scanning

adjust	all-in-one	at	preview (or prescan)
brightness	connected	contrast	file format
flatbed	handheld	high	image editing
low	OCR software	original	click
text	dpi		

How to scan an image

1. Make sure the scanner is _____ to the computer.

2. Lift the lid and put the _____ on the scanner glass.

3. For high image quality, scan _____ 300 _____ or higher.

4. The scanning software will automatically do a _____.

5. If the image is too dark or too light, you can _____ the _____ and _____.

6. _____ "scan".

7. If you scanned _____, it can be "read" by _____.

8. If you want to save the image, choose a _____. JPEG is a good choice for photos.

9. The scanned image can be manipulated using _____ software.

10. An _____ printer/scanner can print, scan and copy.

11. Picture A is a _____ scanner.

12. Picture B is a _____ scanner.

13. Picture C is a _____ resolution photograph.

14. Picture D is a _____ resolution photograph.

dpi stands for dots per inch (1 inch = 2.4cm)

OCR stands for Optical Character Recognition

JPEG is pronounced "jay-peg"

For reference see A & C Black *Dictionary of Computing* (978 07475 6622 9).

Choose the best adjective.

1. Oh dear. I pressed the _____ button.
   a. incorrect   **b.** wrong   **c.** false

2. I can't use my mobile phone. The battery's _____.
   a. over   **b.** flat   **c.** exhausted

3. The battery isn't completely flat, but its very _____.
   a. down   **b.** short   **c.** low

4. My video camera is very _____.
   a. easy to use   **b.** uncomplicated   **c.** obvious

5. My new computer has a very _____ processor.
   a. quick   **b.** high speed   **c.** fast

6. The X19 notebook computer features a very _____ design.
   a. compact   **b.** little   **c.** small

7. Keeping files on paper is _____ solution.
   a. an old-tech   **b.** a past-tech   **c.** a low-tech

8. Keeping files on a computer database is a _____ solution.
   a. new-tech   **b.** now-tech   **c.** high-tech

9. My new PDA is the _____ model.
   a. latest   **b.** newest   **c.** most modern

10. In our office, we've set up a _____ network.
    a. wire-free   **b.** no wires   **c.** wireless

11. A call from New York to Toyko is _____ distance.
    a. far   **b.** long   **c.** faraway

12. I don't think this printer is _____ with my computer.
    a. compatible   **b.** connectable   **c.** suitable

13. My laptop is only 3 centimetres _____.
    a. thick   **b.** tall   **c.** wide

14. The screen on my laptop isn't very _____.
    a. light   **b.** white   **c.** bright

15. In three or four years, my new computer will probably be _____.
    a. old fashioned   **b.** behind the times   **c.** obsolete

16. When you connect this to your computer, it will work immediately. It's _____.
    a. plug and go   **b.** plug and play   **c.** plug and use

For reference see A & C Black *Dictionary of Computing* (978 07475 6622 9).

1.8 Printing

A. Put the words in the spaces.

cartridge	collate	cover	feed
double-sided	landscape	mono	out
out of	portrait	jammed	print-heads
reload	replacement	via	

1. When the ink runs out, you have to change the _____.

2. _____ cartridges can be ordered online.

3. To change the cartridge, you have to lift the _____.

4. The printer is connected to the computer _____ a USB cable.

5. The printer is _____ paper. _____ the paper tray.

6. I think some paper is _____ inside the printer.

7. My printer keeps getting jammed. I think there's a problem with the paper _____.

8. Shall I print this _____ in colour or black and white?

9. "Black and white" is also known as _____.

10. If there's a problem with the print quality, perhaps the _____ need cleaning.

11. Can your printer do _____ printing?

12. To _____ means to put all the pages into the correct order.

13. This page is in _____ orientation.

14. This page is in _____ orientation.

For reference see A & C Black *Dictionary of Computing* (978 07475 6622 9).

B. Which type of printer is each sentence about?

inkjet printer   laser printer

	inkjet printer	laser printer
1. cheaper to buy	✗	
2. cheaper to run		
3. faster printing speed		
4. takes up more space		
5. uses liquid ink		
6. uses toner		
7. more reliable		
8. cartridges need changing more often		

C. True or false?

1.	Inkjet cartridges can be refilled up to three times.	TRUE / FALSE
2.	Colour images are printed by mixing red, green and yellow ink.	TRUE / FALSE
3.	"ppm" stands for pages per minute.	TRUE / FALSE
4.	Most inkjet printers can print out at 100 ppm or more.	TRUE / FALSE
5.	Inkjet cartridges are very difficult to change.	TRUE / FALSE
6.	Photo-paper is a lot more expensive than plain paper.	TRUE / FALSE
7.	Recycled paper is made out of old bottles.	TRUE / FALSE
8.	Some Inkjet printers have three print qualities: draft, normal and best.	TRUE / FALSE
9.	Before you can use a new printer, you have to install the driver from a CD-ROM.	TRUE / FALSE
10.	When a print job has started, it can't be cancelled.	TRUE / FALSE

For reference see A & C Black *Dictionary of Computing* (978 07475 6622 9).

1.9 Mobile Phones

earpiece

hash key

keypad

microphone

(or **mouthpiece**)

screen

star key

Mobile Phone networks

contract	**installed**	**networks**	**operators**
pay-as-you-go	**SIM card**	**roaming**	**tariffs**
top up	**users**		

In Britain there are several mobile phone ¹_____ including Vodaphone, O2, T-mobile and Orange. There are also ²_____ like Virgin Mobile who use the network of another company.

When you buy a cell phone, you have a choice of ³_____. The most popular is "⁴_____", with customers paying for their calls in advance. They can ⁵_____ their accounts in shops, over the internet, and at cash machines. Heavy ⁶_____ may prefer a ⁷_____. They pay a fixed amount every month, but the calls are much cheaper than they are for pay-as-you-go customers.

Mobile phones usually come with a ⁸_____ already ⁹_____. If you take the phone abroad, you may be able to use it on a local network. This is called "¹⁰_____". It can be expensive, and it may be cheaper to buy a foreign SIM card.

For reference see A & C Black *Dictionary of Computing* (978 07475 6622 9).

Choose the best word.

1. After 6pm, calls cost 20p _____ minute
    a. for one   **b.** per   **c.** each

2. You can't use a mobile in a cave because there's no _____.
    a. network   **b.** connection   **c.** power

3. I need to charge up my mobile phone battery. Have you seen my _____?
    a. charger   **b.** recharger   **c.** charging machine

4. When you send a text message, the _____ function can help your write it more quickly.
    a. predicting text   **b.** predictive text   **c.** text predictor

5. In the car, it's safer to use a _____ phone.
    a. handless   **b.** no hands   **c.** hands-free

6. If you don't want to dial a number by mistake, turn on the _____.
    a. keypad locker   **b.** keypad lock   **c.** locker of keypad

7. Which network has the lowest _____?
    a. call charges   **b.** call costs   **c.** call expenses

8. My pay-as-you-go account _____ is about £7.
    a. balance   **b.** level   **c.** amount

9. My average call _____ is about two minutes.
    a. time   **b.** length   **c.** duration

10. We're a long way from the nearest _____ …
    a. broadcaster   **b.** antenna   **c.** transmitter

11. …so the _____ is very weak.
    a. sign   **b.** signal   **c.** transmission

Which is <u>not</u> possible?

12. I'll call her on my…
    a. mobile phone   **b.** cell phone   **c.** moving phone   **d.** cellular phone

13. A mobile phone can't work without a…
    a. SIM card   **b.** sim card   **c.** sim chip   **d.** similar card

14. Don't forget to send me…
    a. a text message   **b.** a text   **c.** an SMS   **d.** a phone message

15. When I arrive, I'll…
    a. text you   **b.** textualise you   **c.** send you an SMS   **d.** send you a text

For reference see A & C Black *Dictionary of Computing* (978 07475 6622 9).

1.10 Other devices

A. Match the devices with the places you would find them.

1.	cash dispenser / cash machine / ATM	a.	at a supermarket checkout
2.	barcode reader	b.	connected to a pair of headphones
3.	magnetic strip	c.	in an office in 1975
4.	MP3 player	d.	in an office, school or copy shop
5.	photocopier	e.	in the hands of a tourist
6.	telex machine	f.	in the headquarters of a large company
7.	video camera	g.	on the back of a credit card
8.	mainframe computer	h.	outside a bank

B. Choose the best word.

9. When you pay by credit card, your card is _____.

    a. swooped   **b.** swiped   **c.** swapped

10. A laptop computer with a screen you can write on is called a _____.

    a. tablet PC   **b.** table PC   **c.** flat screen PC

11. An image on TV or computer screen is made up of thousands of _____.

    a. points   **b.** pixels   **c.** bits

12. You can draw directly onto a computer screen with a _____.

    a. bright pen   **b.** light pen   **c.** pixel pen

13. A camera connected directly to the internet is called _____.

    a. an internet camera   **b.** a web watcher

    c. a webcam

14. The woman in the photo is wearing a _____.

    a. headpiece   **b.** headphone

    c. headset

15. She talks to customers on the telephone all day. She works in a _____.

    a. telephone centre   **b.** call centre

    c. talking centre

For reference see A & C Black *Dictionary of Computing* (978 07475 6622 9).

A. Processors and memory

chips	dual core	megabytes	megahertz
motherboard	processor	speed	upgraded

The "brain" of a computer is the [1]_____. Most of these are made by Intel and AMD, and are sometimes referred to as "[2]_____". The fastest processors are [3]_____, which means that there are two processors working together. The [4]_____ of a processor is measured in [5]_____, which is usually written as MHz.

A computer's memory is measured in [6]_____. If a computer has 1,024 megabytes of memory, and the memory type is SDRAM, this is written as 1,024 MB SDRAM, and is pronounced "a thousand and twenty-four megabytes ess-dee-dram".

The processor and memory modules are located on the [7]_____. Changing a computer's processor is not generally practical, but the memory can usually be [8]_____.

B. Power

disconnect	fan	mains electricity
overheating	shock	spikes
supply	surge protector	transformer

1. Laptops are powered by batteries or _____.

2. Mains electricity is converted to lower voltage by a _____.

3. A _____ protects electronic equipment from damage caused by power _____.

4. If you remove the cover from a computer, make sure you _____ the electricity _____. Otherwise, you may get an electric _____.

5. The computer is cooled by a _____. This prevents the processor from _____.

For reference see A & C Black *Dictionary of Computing* (978 07475 6622 9).

1.12 Data storage

burn	capacity	card	drawer
eject	free space	hard drive	stick

1. The data and applications on your computer are stored on the _____.

2. To run this application you need at least 50MB of _____ on your hard drive.

3. My computer's hard drive has a _____ of 120GB.

4. Do you like this CD? I can _____ you a copy if you want.

5. The opposite of "Insert the DVD" is "_____ the DVD".

6. I can't eject the CD. I think the _____'s stuck.

7. Digital cameras usually store pictures on a memory _____ or a memory _____.

Which do you think is the *best* solution for each problem? (More than one solution is possible for some of problems.)

1. I want to make a copy of a music CD.

2. I want to store some files. I may need to update them in the future.

3. I want to back up data from my computer. I want to update it every day.

4. My computer's having problems with reading and writing CDs.

5. I want to add 100MB of extra storage to my computer.

6. I want to send a copy of a small file to a friend. He has an old computer.

7. My computer's running slowly.

a. You need an **external hard drive**.

b. Use a **CD-R**.

c. Try a **USB flash drive**.

d. Perhaps you need a new internal CD drive.

e. Put them on a **CD-RW**.

f. Perhaps you need to **defragment** the hard drive.

g. You could put it on a **floppy disk**.

For reference see A & C Black *Dictionary of Computing* (978 07475 6622 9).

1. Scanners, printers and webcams are _____.

    a. extras   **b.** peripherals   **c.** externals

2. Add extra USB _____ to your computer....

    a. ports   **b.** doors   **c.** windows

3. ... with a USB _____.

    a. centre   **b.** point   **c.** hub

4. ADSL is also known as _____.

    a. wideband   **b.** broadband   **c.** longband

5. I want to get a _____ ADSL modem.

    a. quick-speed   **b.** fast-speed   **c.** high-speed

6. The internet is much faster with a broadband connection than with _____.

    a. dial-up   **b.** phone-up   **c.** call-up

7. With a wireless router, you can _____ your broadband connection with other users.

    a. divide   **b.** combine   **c.** share

8. This wire's too short. I need an _____ cable.

    a. extended   **b.** extension   **c.** extender

9. You can connect a USB plug to a PS/2 port by using _____.

    a. an adaptor   **b.** a bridge   **c.** a connector

Bluetooth®

data	**developed**	**devices**	**enabled**
signals	**wireless**	**telecommunications**	

Bluetooth® technology enables [1]_____ communication between [2]_____ such as laptop computers, mobile phones and PDAs. Bluetooth® [3]_____ devices use short-range radio [4]_____ to exchange [5]_____ quickly and easily. The technology was [6]_____ by a group of computer and [7]_____ companies including IBM, Intel, Nokia and Ericsson.

For reference see A & C Black *Dictionary of Computing* (978 07475 6622 9).

1.14 Networks

LAN

intranet	Local	log onto	network card
satellite	server	terminals	WAN (Wide Area Network)

LAN is pronounced "lan", and stands for [1]_____ Area Network. In a typical LAN, there is a central network [2]_____ which supports a number of [3]_____. Users have to [4]_____ the network server. Pages of information that can be viewed within a LAN are called an [5]_____. A number of LANs connected to each other via [6]_____ or other form of __communication are called a [7]_____. To be used as network terminals, each computer needs to have a [8]_____ installed.

Network topologies

line (or **bus**)   **ring**   **star**   **hierarchical**

1. _____ topology

2. _____ topology

3. _____ topology

4. _____ topology

For reference see A & C Black *Dictionary of Computing* (978 07475 6622 9).

A. EPOS and EFTPOS

Cross out the incorrect word

EPOS (electronic point of sale) terminals are **cash / money** registers found in retail **openings / outlets** such as shops and restaurants. They are connected to a **central / centre** computer, and data about **objects / goods** and services sold is entered into the terminals via keyboards, barcode readers, **touch / finger** screens etc. They are useful for stock management, and can produce itemised bills and **receipts / recipes**.

EFTPOS (electronic funds transfer point of sale) can also transfer **cash / funds** directly from the customer's bank account via a **debit / paying** card. They are now more common than EPOS terminals.

B. Word partnerships

Match the words.

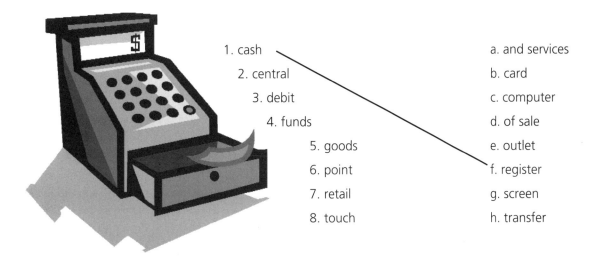

1. cash	a. and services
2. central	b. card
3. debit	c. computer
4. funds	d. of sale
5. goods	e. outlet
6. point	f. register
7. retail	g. screen
8. touch	h. transfer

C. Plastic

Match the cards with the phrases.

1. credit card	a. Buy now, pay now.
2. debit card	b. Buy now, pay the bank later.
3. cash card	c. Buy now, pay the shop later.
4. loyalty card	d. Spend, and get some money or goods back from the shop.
5. store card	e. Take money out of a cash machine.

For reference see A & C Black *Dictionary of Computing* (978 07475 6622 9).

1.16 Review crossword

All the words can be found in Units 1.1 to 1.15

Across

1. A camera connected to the internet. (6 letters)

6. To send an SMS message. (4)

9. The most common page orientation. (8)

10. A computer's "brain". (9)

11. It prevents a computer from overheating. (3)

14. A connection without wires. (7)

15. The place where you put a plug. (6)

20. Processor speeds are measured in these. (9)

21. The cheapest type of printer. (6)

22. Lift this before you use your scanner. (3)

24. The shop assistant does this to your credit card. (5)

26. The strip on the back of a credit or debit card. (8)

Down

2. When it's dead, recharge it or replace it. (7)

3. You speak into this. (10)

4. The mouse moves on this. (3)

5. A computer, printer and scanner on a desk with a chair. (11)

7. Laser printers use this instead of ink. (5)

8. A design (for example, a type of keyboard) which is better for your body. (9)

12. An image on a screen is made up of thousands of these. (6)

13. Printers, scanners, webcams etc. (10)

16. A very large computer which never moves. (9)

17. A photo or drawing. (5)

18. You need to change or refill this when your printer runs out of ink. (9)

19. Two or more computers connected together. (7)

23. The slowest form of internet connection. (4, 2)

26. Image resolution is usually measured in this. (3)

For reference see A & C Black *Dictionary of Computing* (978 07475 6622 9).

For reference see A & C Black *Dictionary of Computing* (978 07475 6622 9).

1.17 Your computer

Can you answer these questions in English?

1. What kind of computer do you have?

_____

_____

_____

2. Do you know the technical specifications of you computer?

_____

_____

_____

3. Would you like to upgrade your computer? If so, what kind of computer would you like to get?

_____

_____

_____

4. Which peripherals do you use most often? Why?

_____

_____

_____

5. Do you use computer networks? If so, how do you connect to the networks you use?

_____

_____

_____

For reference see A & C Black *Dictionary of Computing* (978 07475 6622 9).

Section 2:
Software

2.1 Software: the basics

A. Choose the correct word to fill the spaces.

1. Turn on your computer. It will usually take a few minutes to _____.
   - **a.** boot itself
   - **b.** boot up
   - **c.** get booted

2. Windows XP, Macintosh OSX and Linux are _____.
   - **a.** operating systems
   - **b.** operating tools
   - **c.** operators

3. On my computer, I have a picture of my cat as the _____.
   - **a.** desktop background
   - **b.** desktop picture
   - **c.** desktop scene

4. Microsoft Word, Adobe Acrobat and CorelDraw are programs or _____.
   - **a.** applicators
   - **b.** appliers
   - **c.** applications

5. To open Microsoft Word, click on the _____.
   - **a.** picture
   - **b.** symbol
   - **c.** icon

6. I keep all my digital photos in a _____ called "Photos".
   - **a.** folder
   - **b.** packet
   - **c.** box

7. Is it possible to open Microsoft Excel _____ in Word?
   - **a.** texts
   - **b.** files
   - **c.** pages

8. In Microsoft Word, to start typing a new letter, open a new _____.
   - **a.** document
   - **b.** page
   - **c.** paper

9. When you _____ a document, it's sent to the recycle bin.
   - **a.** destroy
   - **b.** erase
   - **c.** delete

10. Deleted documents stay in the recycle bin until you _____ it.
    - **a.** wash
    - **b.** empty
    - **c.** clean

11. In Windows, the icon is just a _____ to the application. If you delete the icon, the application will still be on your computer.
    - **a.** connector
    - **b.** shortcut
    - **c.** link

12. If the computer crashes, you can try pressing the _____ button.
    - **a.** restart
    - **b.** recommence
    - **c.** replay

13. When I've finished using my computer, I always _____.
    - **a.** close it down
    - **b.** shut it down
    - **c.** shut it off

14. If I leave my computer on without using it, after a while it goes into _____ mode.
    - **a.** stand down
    - **b.** waiting
    - **c.** standby

For reference see A & C Black *Dictionary of Computing* (978 07475 6622 9).

B. Insert the missing words.

close
drag and drop
find
free up
installed
launch
password
renamed
running
save
search
start menu
uninstalling
user
window

1. I couldn't open the document you emailed me. I don't have Microsoft Word _____ on my computer.

2. Click on that icon to _____ Internet Explorer.

3. I _____ an important document, and now I can't find it.

4. If your computer is _____ several applications at the same time, it's more likely to crash. It's better to _____ the applications. you're not using.

5. You can access all the applications on your computer from the _____.

6. You can view two Word documents on the screen at the same time. You just open a new _____.

7. It's easy to move files into a folder. You can just _____.

8. I asked the computer to _____ for files with "English" in the name, but it didn't _____ any.

9. This is a shared computer. Each _____ has their own _____.

10. You can _____ space on your hard drive by _____ applications you never use.

11. If you _____ your photos as JPEGs instead of TIFFs, you'll use a lot less memory.

For reference see A & C Black *Dictionary of Computing* (978 07475 6622 9).

2.2 Using software: useful verbs

Match the words on the left with the words on the right.

Set 1

1. **arrange** the
2. **cut** and **paste**
3. **install**
4. **open** the document in
5. **resize** the
6. **save** it as

a. a Microsoft Word file
b. a new window
c. photo. It's too big.
d. an application
e. some text
f. icons on the desktop

Set 2

1. **copy** the
2. **customize** your
3. **launch**
4. **search**
5. **send** the file
6. **use** the

a. for a lost file
b. a program
c. "search" function
d. text into a new document
e. to a different folder
f. desktop

Set 3

1. accidentally **deleted** an
2. **exit**
3. **click** on that button
4. **pull down** a
5. **replace** the existing
6. **view**

a. menu
b. important file
c. an application
d. as a web page
e. on the task bar
f. file

Set 4

1. **close down** an
2. **log off**
3. **look in**
4. **put** the file
5. **run** a
6. **wipe** the

a. after a session
b. all folders
c. application
d. hard drive
e. on a USB memory key
f. program

For reference see A & C Black *Dictionary of Computing* (978 07475 6622 9).

Write the words into the spaces.

adding	background	~~customising~~
default	digital	displayed
format	image	performance
properties	screen saver	setting up
tasks	wallpaper	wireless

The control panel provides options for [1] **customising** the appearance of your computer screen, [2]_____ or removing programs and [3]_____ network connections.

When you get a new computer, perhaps the first thing you will want to do is set the date and time. You can also choose the [4]_____ for dates and times. For example, November 4th 2007 can be [5]_____ as 04-11-2007, 2007-11-04 or in various other formats.

You may wish to change the desktop [6]_____ to a picture, for example a personal photo taken on a [7]_____ camera. A picture on the desktop background is also known as [8]_____.

If a computer screen shows the same [9]_____ for a very long time, it can leave a permanent impression. To avoid this, you can choose a [10]_____. This is usually a simple moving pattern which activates if the computer is not used for a set amount of time (for example, five minutes).

You can also use the control panel to set up or change internet and other network connections, including [11]_____ network connections.

In fact, you can change most aspects of your computer's [12]_____ through the control panel, such as the system [13]_____, modem settings, scheduled [14]_____, although most users prefer to leave on the [15]_____ settings rather than changing them.

For reference see A & C Black *Dictionary of Computing* (978 07475 6622 9).

2.4 Applications

A. Match the descriptions on the left with these famous applications.

1. word processor	**a.** Adobe Photoshop
2. spreadsheet	**b.** Internet Explorer
3. virus protection	**c.** Microsoft Word
4. browser	**d.** Microsoft Excel
5. image editor	**e.** Microsoft PowerPoint
6. media player	**f.** Norton AntiVirus
7. email software	**g.** Outlook Express
8. presentation software	**h.** Adobe PageMaker
9. graphic design software	**i.** RealPlayer

B. Crossword

1. programs which tell the computer what to do (8)

2. a piece of software which makes a computer do a task (for example, edit an image) (11)

3. any set of instructions for a computer (7)

4. software which operates a peripheral, such as a scanner or printer (6)

5. application which stores and displays digital photos (5,5)

6. you enter a security code to prove that you have a _____ to use the software (7)

7. software which prevents unauthorised access to your computer over the internet (8)

8. a series of letters and numbers which you have to enter before installing some programs (8,4)

9. download new features for an application (6)

10. an unauthorised copy of a program (7)

For reference see A & C Black *Dictionary of Computing* (978 07475 6622 9).

A. Choose the best words.

1. Software which is easy to use is…
   - **a.** user-easy
   - **b.** user-friendly
   - **c.** usable

2. Software which is obvious to use is…
   - **a.** intuitive
   - **b.** guessable
   - **c.** comprehensible

3. Software which is not obvious to use is…
   - **a.** counter-intuitive
   - **b.** unintuitive
   - **c.** non-intuitive

4. Software for use by children and schools is…
   - **a.** learning
   - **b.** teaching
   - **c.** educational

5. Software for use by businesses is…
   - **a.** commercial
   - **b.** businesslike
   - **c.** busy

6. Software made specially for one company is…
   - **a.** one-off
   - **b.** unique
   - **c.** tailor-made

7. Software for use at home is…
   - **a.** for home use
   - **b.** for house use…
   - **c.** for household use

8. Software which has been illegally copied is…
   - **a.** unreal
   - **b.** pirated
   - **c.** fake

9. Software which has been bought from the company that produced it is…
   - **a.** real
   - **b.** justified
   - **c.** licensed

Types of software

B. Match the type of software with the definition.

1. trial version

2. shareware

3. freeware

4. home-use version

5. professional version

a. A **simplified** version which is cheaper to buy.

b. Software which is in the **public domain**. Anybody can use it without paying.

c. The **full version** with all the features.

d. You can try it for a while for free. Then if you want to keep using it, you are expected to pay a small **fee** to the writer.

e. You can use it for free for a while (often a month). When the **trial period** finishes, you have to pay, or the program will **de-activate**.

For reference see A & C Black *Dictionary of Computing* (978 07475 6622 9).

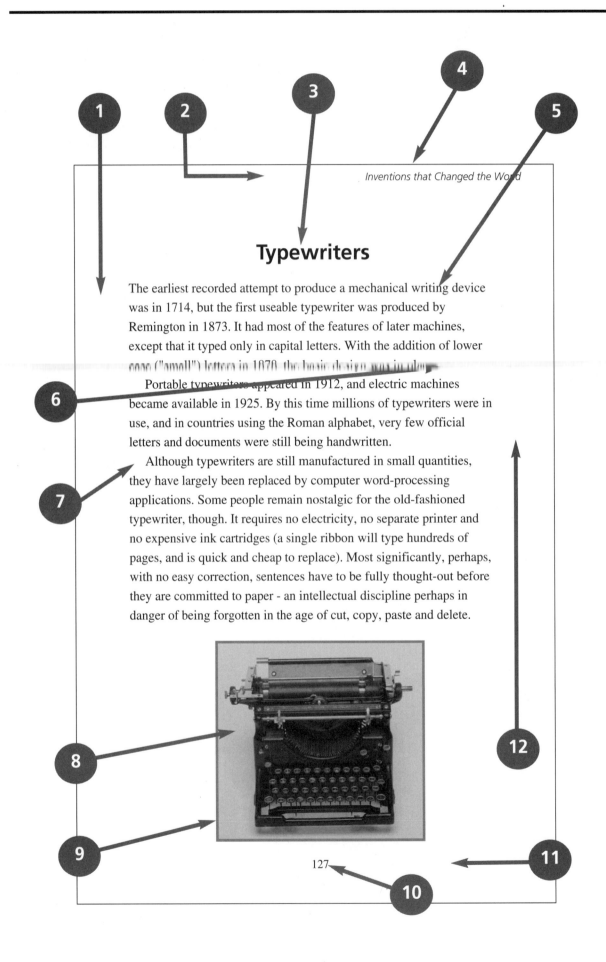

Inventions that Changed the Word

Typewriters

The earliest recorded attempt to produce a mechanical writing device was in 1714, but the first useable typewriter was produced by Remington in 1873. It had most of the features of later machines, except that it typed only in capital letters. With the addition of lower case ("small") letters in 1878, the basic design was in place.

Portable typewriters appeared in 1912, and electric machines became available in 1925. By this time millions of typewriters were in use, and in countries using the Roman alphabet, very few official letters and documents were still being handwritten.

Although typewriters are still manufactured in small quantities, they have largely been replaced by computer word-processing applications. Some people remain nostalgic for the old-fashioned typewriter, though. It requires no electricity, no separate printer and no expensive ink cartridges (a single ribbon will type hundreds of pages, and is quick and cheap to replace). Most significantly, perhaps, with no easy correction, sentences have to be fully thought-out before they are committed to paper - an intellectual discipline perhaps in danger of being forgotten in the age of cut, copy, paste and delete.

127

For reference see A & C Black *Dictionary of Computing* (978 07475 6622 9).

A. Write the numbers next to the words.

2	top margin
	bottom margin
	left-hand margin
	right-hand margin
	heading (or title)
	body text
	paragraph break
	indent
	illustration
	border (or frame)
	page number
	page border (or edge of the page)

B. Match the words with the types of lettering

bold   bold italic   italic

lower case (or small letters)

outline   plain text   shadow

strikethrough   underline

upper case (or capital letters)

1. _____ ABCDEFG

2. _____ abcdefg

3. _____ Typewriters

4. _____ **Typewriters**

5. _____ *Typewriters*

6. _____ ***Typewriters***

7. _____ T̲y̲p̲e̲w̲r̲i̲t̲e̲r̲s̲

8. _____ ~~Typewriters~~

9. _____ Typewriters

10. _____ **Typewriters**

C. Choose the best words.

1. The text about typewriters is divided into three _____.

    a. sections   **b.** paragraphs   **c.** chunks

2. Times, Arial and Courier are types of _____.

    a. lettering   **b.** character   **c.** font

3. The text about typewriters is _____.

    a. single spaced   **b.** double spaced   **c.** one-and-half spaced

4. "Inventions that Changed the World" is the _____.

    a. header   **b.** footer   **c.** footnote

5. Do you think the margins are too _____ or _____?

    a. big / small   **b.** wide / narrow   **c.** long / short

6. Do you like the page _____?

    a. layout   **b.** organisation   **c.** pattern

For reference see A & C Black *Dictionary of Computing* (978 07475 6622 9).

Sunnydays Coach Tours

Winter / Spring Tours

Dec 1st: *Paris*
Five nights in a four star hotel just 200 metres from the Eiffel
Towers. All meals included. Depart London 10 am.

Dec 7th: *Amsterdam*
Three nights in simple guest house overlooking a canal in
the heart of Amsterdam. Breakfast and a canal tour included
in the price. Depart 8.00 am Bristol, 10.15 am London.

Dec 11th / Dec 16th: *Christmas Markets in Vienna*
Discover the magic of Austria's Christmas markets. Five
nights half-board. Optional extra trip to Innsbruck. Depart
Cardiff 8 am Dec 11th, and London 9 am Dec 16th.

Dec 29th: *New Year in Verona*
Three nights half board in one of northern Italy's most
beautiful cities. On the evening of Dec 31st enjoy a five
course gourmet meal in one of Verona's finest restaurants,
followed by the traditional firework display in Piazza Bra.

January 13th to March 10th: *Skiing in the French Alps*
Avoid the airport crowds – go by coach! Departures
Saturdays 9am London. Drop-off points throughout SW
France. Wide range of accommodation packages available.

March 20th / March 27th: Berlin
Five nights full board in a two star
hotel conveniently located a short
metro ride from the city centre.
Price includes a three-day travel
pass. Depart 8.00 am Bristol,
10.15 am London

April 4th: *Easter in San Sebastian*
Enjoy the traditional Easter celebrations in one of northern
Spain's most elegant and
atmospheric cities. 6 nights half board in a three star sea-
front hotel.
Depart London 8.30 am.

April 11th / April 17th : *The Tulip Fields of Holland*
Experience the beauty of rural Holland in spring, based in a
comfortable guesthouse in the historic city of Delft. Five
nights half board. Depart Cardiff 8 am April 11th, and
London 9 am April 17th.

April 24th: *Barcelona*
Five nights in a centrally-located one-star hotel on a bed-
and-breakfast basis. Price includes a three-day city
transport card. Optional extra excursion to the Salvador Dali
museum in Figueres. Depart London 8 am

A. Choose the best words.

1. "Winter / Spring Tours" is the _____.
   - **a.** under-heading
   - **b.** sub-heading
   - **c.** below-heading

2. The body text is divided into two _____.
   - **a.** columns
   - **b.** pillars
   - **c.** strips

3. The body text is _____.
   - **a.** left-aligned
   - **b.** centred
   - **c.** justified

4. The illustration isn't original artwork. It's _____.
   - **a.** screen art
   - **b.** free art
   - **c.** clipart

5. The clipart has been given _____.
   - **a.** an under shadow
   - **b.** a drop shadow
   - **c.** a sub-shadow

6. This poster has been given a 10% grey background _____.
   - **a.** wash
   - **b.** fill
   - **c.** colour

7. The design of this poster is _____.
   - **a.** a bit amateurish
   - **b.** highly professional
   - **c.** state-of-the-art

For reference see A & C Black *Dictionary of Computing* (978 07475 6622 9).

Punctuation and symbols

B. Match the words with the punctuation marks and symbols.

1. full stop	a.	!
2. comma	b.	@
3. exclamation mark	c.	,
4. question mark	d.	&
5. single quotes	e.	.
6. double quotes	f.	=
7. dollar sign	g.	'Hello'
8. percentage sign	h.	→
9. ampersand	i.	*
10. asterisk	j.	"Hello"
11. hash	k.	_
12. brackets	l.	-
13. left bracket	m.	?
14. square brackets	n.	/
15. underscore	o.	( )
16. hyphen	p.	$
17. plus sign	q.	\
18. equals sign	r.	[ ]
19. colon	s.	%
20. semicolon	t.	(
21. "at" sign	u.	#
22. forward slash	v.	:
23. backward slash	w.	+
24. arrow	x.	;

C. Look at this table, and answer true or false.

Departure times

Bristol	London	Dover
8.15	10.30	12.45
14.00	16.15	18.30
17.45	19.00	21.15

1. All the cells are the same size.

2. There are four columns and three rows.

3. The text in the top bar is reversed-out.

4. The middle column has a lighter flood fill.

5. The text is centred within its cells.

6. The table gridlines are grey.

For reference see A & C Black *Dictionary of Computing* (978 07475 6622 9).

2.8 Word processing 3

A. Match the word processing tool with the task.

1. word count   **a.** produces form letters and address labels

2. spell checker   **b.** counts the number of words, lines and paragraphs

3. auto format   **c.** finds all instances of a word or phrases in a document

4. template   **d.** checks the text for spelling errors

5. find   **e.** automatically changes the styles of headings, lists etc.

6. replace   **f.** shows how a document has been altered

7. print preview   **g.** records a sequence of commands, and applies them when required

8. track changes   **h.** a pre-formatted blank document – just type your text into the fields

9. mail merge   **i.** shows how the document will look in print

10. macro   **j.** replaces words or phrases in a document with new text

B. Match the words with the examples.

1. Times 10 point

2. Times 24 point

3. bullet points

4. superscript

5. subscript

6. justified text

7. highlighted text

8. text wrap

a. Jane stared at the screen

b. Jane stared at the screen. The document had disappeared! She hadn't made a back-up copy. Hours of work wasted!

c. Possible courses of action:
- Re-type the entire document.
- Get a computer engineer to find if the text could be retrieved.
- Resign, and get another job.

d. Jane stared at the screen.

e. Jane stared at the screen.

f. Jan. 24th

g. A_2

h. Jane stared at the screen. The document had disappeared! She hadn't made a back-up copy. Hours of work wasted!

For reference see A & C Black *Dictionary of Computing* (978 07475 6622 9).

C. True or false?

1. This text has been rotated 45 degrees anti-clockwise. ⟶

2. This text box has no border.

3. This is an AutoShape with a 2pt black border and a 30% grey fill.

4. These are types of callout.

ROTATED TEXT

Voice balloon

Thought bubble

Jane stared at the screen. The document had disappeared! She hadn't made a back-up copy. Hours of work wasted!

D. Choose the best words.

1. Making changes to a text is called _____.
   a. altering   **b.** renewing   **c.** editing

2. To change normal text to italic, first you must _____ the text you want to format.
   a. choose   **b.** take   **c.** select

3. A very pale image behind the text is called _____.
   a. an ink mark   **b.** a watermark   **c.** a grey mark

4. To divide the text into two pages, insert a _____.
   a. page break   **b.** page stop   **c.** page change

5. The numbers at the bottom of the page are _____.
   a. page numbers   **b.** sheet numbers   **c.** paper numbers

6. An extra note at the bottom of the page (usually in a smaller font size) is called a _____.
   a. bottom note   **b.** foot   **c.** footnote

7. In word processing, to put things into alphabetical order is to _____.
   a. sort   **b.** organise   **c.** order

8. A list of contacts, addresses etc. is called _____.
   a. an archive   **b.** a list   **c.** a database

9. Producing a document on your computer and sending it direct to a printing press is _____.
   a. computer publishing   **b.** desktop publishing   **c.** electronic publishing

10. Cut or copied text is temporarily stored in the _____.
   a. clipboard   **b.** clip   **c.** clipart

39

2.9 Image editing

A. Match the word with the definition.

1. crop	**a.** turn an image
2. sharpen	**b.** reverse an image
3. soften	**c.** improve the appearance of an image
4. zoom in	**d.** remove part of an image
5. zoom out	**e.** copy part of an image to another point in that image
6. flip	**f.** view part of the image in more detail
7. rotate	**g.** view more of the image in less detail
8. touch up	**h.** convert a vector image to a bitmap image (see B5 below)
9. clone	**i.** make the image less blurred
10. rasterize	**j.** make the image more blurred

B. True or false?

1. Greyscale images take up more disk space than **colour** images.

2. It's often preferable to scan **line drawings** as **black and white images** rather than greyscale images. This takes up less disk space, and produces sharper lines. This type of image is also known as **lineart**.

3. On most computers, you can view photos as a **slideshow** – each photo is shown for a few seconds.

4. You can also view photos as **fingernails** – small versions of the photos, with lots shown on the screen at the same time.

5. A **vector image** (for example, a **clipart** image) can be expanded to any size without loss of **resolution**. A **bitmap image** (for example, a photo) is made of **pixels**, so it loses resolution when it is expanded.

greyscale

black and white

high contrast

high brightness

For reference see A & C Black *Dictionary of Computing* (978 07475 6622 9).

Choose the best words from each pair in **bold**.

1. It's usually possible to [1] **import / introduce** Adobe PageMaker files into Adobe InDesign. The majority of graphic design applications can [2] **export / send off** documents as PDF files, or as HTML web pages.

2. This box has a black [3] **frame / outside**, also known as a "stroke". Inside the frame, the fill is a [4] **fade / gradient** from dark grey to light grey.

The difference between the two versions of "wave", is that [5] **curling / kerning** has been applied to the top version.

3. A frame, graphic or block of text is known as [6] **an object / a thing**. These are arranged in [7] **levels / layers** – the top layer [8] **overlaps / overruns** the layer below.

4. This image is [9] **blurred / soft** at the edges (see unit 1.6 for the original). This [10] **result / effect** is also known as [11] **feathering / birding**.

5. [12] **Full bleed / total bleed** means that the page is printed right up to the edges – there are no white margins. The [13] **snail / slug** area is the area outside the area to be printed where instructions for the printer are written.

6. This image has been [14] **pulled / stretched** (see unit 2.8 for the original).

7. Before a document goes [15] **to press / for printing**, it's essential to check the [16] **examples / proofs** for errors.

8. Like desktop printers, most colour printing [17] **machines / presses** print in four colours: cyan (light blue), magenta (dark pink), yellow and black. Before printing, a document must be divided into the four colours. this process is called colour [18] **separation / division**. These separations are then turned into [19] **plates / stamps** – one for each of the inks that will be used.

9. Prior to colour separation, coloured images, graphics and text have to be [20] **transformed / converted** from RGB (Red Green Blue), the colour format of computer displays, to CMYK (Cyan Magenta Yellow Black) the colour format of printing presses.

10. The process of preparing documents from a graphic designer for the printing press is called [21] **reprographics / reproduction**.

For reference see A & C Black *Dictionary of Computing* (978 07475 6622 9).

2.11 Spreadsheets

	A	B	C	D	E	F	G
1							
2							
3							
4							
5							
6							

A. Choose the best word.

1. A basic spreadsheet is a _____ of spaces for data.
   a. grid   **b.** cage   **c.** ladder

2. A spreadsheet consists of columns and _____.
   a. lengths   **b.** lines   **c.** rows

3. A spreadsheet grid is called a worksheet. A file containing one or more worksheets is called a _____.
   a. workout   **b.** work   **c.** workbook

4. In the worksheet above, the _____ cell is in column B, row 3.
   a. important   **b.** active   **c.** focus

5. Use the mouse pointer to select a single cell or _____ of cells.
   a. bunch   **b.** group   **c.** block

6. It's easy to adjust the column _____.
   a. size   **b.** width   **c.** space

7. Spreadsheets can perform mathematical _____.
   a. calculations   **b.** deductions   **c.** jobs

8. To get a worksheet to perform a mathematical calculation, you have to enter a _____.
   a format   **b.** form   **c.** formula

9. A number in a spreadsheet cell is often called a _____.
   a. digit   **b.** numeral   **c.** value

10. To remove the contents of a cell is to _____ that cell.
    a. clean   **b.** wash   **c.** clear

11. To remove a complete row is to _____ that row.
    a. wipe   **b.** delete   **c.** erase

12. Changing the fonts, colours etc. of a spreadsheet is called _____.
    a. formatting   **b.** forming   **c.** reforming

42

For reference see A & C Black *Dictionary of Computing* (978 07475 6622 9).

B. Add the arithmetic operator symbols to the table below.

*   /   ^   -   +

symbol	verb	noun	everyday speech
	add	addition	"five plus three equals eight"
	subtract	subtraction	"five minus three equals two"
	multiply	multiplication	"five multiplied by three equals fifteen" "five times three equals fifteen"
	divide	division	"fifteen divided by three equals five"
	raise to the power of		"ten to the power of five is 100,000"

C. Answer true or false.

0.75 → 7.5

1. The decimal point has been shifted one place to the right.   **TRUE / FALSE**

188
102
65
12

2. The four numbers above have been sorted in ascending order.   **TRUE / FALSE**

0.005
0.05
5,000
5,055.5

3. The four numbers above have been sorted in descending order.   **TRUE / FALSE**

apples
bananas
pears
pineapples

4. The four words above have been sorted in alphabetical order.   **TRUE / FALSE**

D. Choose the best words from each pair in grey type.

Three useful features in Microsoft Excel:

- Cells can contain [1] **text / language**, numerical [2] **values / details** and formulas. It's also possible to add pop-up comment [3] **boxes / squares** containing additional information (choose **Comment** from the **Insert** menu).

- The **Fill** and **Autofill** commands can be used for making multiple copies of the contents of a cell. Autofill can also be used to automatically create a [4] **list / series** of months, numbers etc.

- You can improve the [5] **looks / appearance** of a spreadsheet very quickly by using the **AutoFormat** feature.

For reference see A & C Black *Dictionary of Computing* (978 07475 6622 9).

2.12 Presentation software

1. In Microsoft PowerPoint, when creating a new presentation, you can choose between a blank presentation, a design template and the AutoContent _____.

    a. witch   **b.** wizard   **c.** bogeyman

2. PowerPoint can be used to create presentation _____.

    a. slideshows   **b.** picture shows   **c.** exhibitions

3. You can choose a _____ to move from one slide to another.

    a. changing effect   **b.** moving effect   **c.** transition effect

4. You can include moving pictures in your presentation. These are called _____.

    a. films   **b.** movies   **c.** animations

5. You can choose a _____ for your presentation.

    a. colour pattern   **b.** colour arrangement   **c.** colour scheme

6. You can give your presentation over the internet as an _____.

    a. online broadcast   **b.** online show   **c.** online spectacle

7. It's usually clearer to present statistics in the form of a table or _____.

    a. chart   **b.** figure   **c.** track

8. If you wish, the software will help you _____ of your presentation.

    a. practice the times   **b.** rehearse the timing   **c.** try out the times

9. You can choose to record the _____ on your computer…

    a. narration   **b.** speaking   **c.** voice

10. …rather than giving it _____.

    a. in real life   **b.** for real   **c.** live

For reference see A & C Black *Dictionary of Computing* (978 07475 6622 9).

Choose the correct preposition. Then match the problem with the solution.

1. The operating system **in / on** my computer doesn't support the latest version **of / from** this application.

2. These files are too big.

3. My computer says it hasn't got enough memory **for / to** run this program.

4. I can't understand this program. It's too complicated.

5. I think there's a bug **in / inside** this software.

6. There doesn't seem to be an icon for the program **in / on** the desktop.

7. I can't use this program. It's all **in / with** French!

8. I can't get the driver for my new printer **to / at** work.

9. I haven't got a media player **in / on** my computer.

a. You can download one for free **to / from** the internet.

b. Perhaps you could get an older version – or buy a new computer!

c. What about uninstalling the driver for your old printer?

d. Have you checked to see if there are any updates available **in / on** the internet?

e. Why don't you close **off / down** all those other applications you've got open?

f. You can get a manual. I've seen one in the local bookshop.

g. How about compressing them **with / by** WinZip?

h. Go **to / on** the "start" menu, and click **at / on** "All Programs".

i. Change the language setting.

1. ___	2. ___	3. ___	4. ___	5. ___	6. ___	7. ___	8. ___	9. ___

For reference see A & C Black *Dictionary of Computing* (978 07475 6622 9).

2.14 Which program?

Match the operations with the application types.

	word processor	spreadsheet	image editor	media player
1. select text	x	x		
2. save as JPEG				
3. insert table				
4. play				
5. touch up				
6. import photo				
7. exit				
8. copy from CD				
9. check internet for updates				
10. copy a block of cells				
11. insert text box				
12. page set-up				
13. optimise for internet				
14. uninstall				
15. add border				
16. insert bullet points				
17. convert to MP3				
18. paste into new document				
19. check spelling				
20. change text direction				
21. flip, crop and rotate				
22. sort				
23. alter formula values				
24. create playlist				
25. print				
26. clear all cells				
27. maximise window				
28. insert column break				
29. convert to greyscale				
30. open				

For reference see A & C Black *Dictionary of Computing* (978 07475 6622 9).

1. Can you name three operating systems?

2. Where do deleted documents go?

3. What's another word for the desktop background? (It begins with W.)

4. Where do you go to customise the appearance and other settings of your computer?

5. What type of application can be used to touch up photos?

6. What type of application can be used to store and play music?

7. What do you call software that can be used by anybody without a licence?

8. How would you describe this text?

REVISION QUIZ

9. Which will fit more text onto a page, Arial 9 point double spaced, or Arial 36 point single spaced?

10. What do you call a pre-formatted blank document?

11. Where is a section of cut or copied text (or image) temporarily stored?

12. How is a flipped image different to the original?

13. What's the opposite of sharpening an image?

14. What do you call very small versions of images?

15. What word means to put in alphabetical or numerical order?

16. What do you call one box in a table or spreadsheet?

17. What word beginning with S means a series of displays in a presentation?

18. What do you call a small technical problem in a piece of software?

19. What does WinZip do? (Clue: is the file too big?)

20. What kind of software operates printers, scanners etc?

21. Tables and spreadsheet grids are made up of _____ (vertical) and _____ (horizontal).

22 to 30. Can you name these symbols?

22. **$** 23. **&** 24. ***** 25. **#** 26. **( )** 27. **/** 28. **** 29. **?** 30. **+**

For reference see A & C Black *Dictionary of Computing* (978 07475 6622 9).

2.16 Your software

Can you answer these questions in English?

1. Which application do you use most often? Why?

_____

_____

_____

2. How does it help you in your work?

_____

_____

_____

3. Which features do you find most useful?

_____

_____

_____

4. Does it have any limitations which annoy you? What are they?

_____

_____

_____

5. Is there an application you'd like to learn to use? What would you use it for?

_____

_____

_____

And this disk is the tutorial on how to use the tutorial disk.

For reference see A & C Black *Dictionary of Computing* (978 07475 6622 9).

Section 3:
The Internet

3.1 The internet: the basics

A. Choose the best word from each pair in *grey* type.

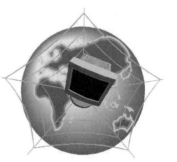

What's the difference between the Web and the internet?

Some people think that the internet and the Web are the same thing, but in fact they are different. The internet (often called simply "the net") is a global [1] **network** / **net** of interconnected computers. These computers communicate with each other [2] **over** / **through** existing telecommunications networks – principally, the telephone system. The Word Wide Web (usually known as just "the Web") is the billions of web pages that are stored on large computers called web [3] **servers** / **services**.

To [4] **see** / **access** the web, you need a computer and a modem. You then connect over your telephone line to an internet service [5] **port** / **provider** (ISP), which sends your request to view a particular web page to the correct web server.

Websites are not the only service available on the internet. It is also used for many other functions, including sending and receiving email, and connecting to newsgroups and [6] **discussion** / **talking** groups.

You could say that the internet is a system of roads, and web pages and emails are types of traffic that travel on those roads.

B. Put these operations in the order that you do them (variations are possible).

	close down your browser
	connect to your ISP
	disconnect from the internet
	enter a web address (also known as a URL*) into the address field
	launch your browser (for example, Internet Explorer, Netscape Navigator or Mozilla Firefox)
	perhaps wait for a few seconds while the web-page downloads
	view the page

* URL stands for Uniform Resource Locator, but the full term is almost never used

Web addresses

Web address / URL:	**http://www.acblack.co.uk**
domain name	**www.acblack.co.uk**
host:	**acblack**
protocol:	**http://**
type of site:	**.co.uk**
country code:	**.uk**

For reference see A & C Black *Dictionary of Computing* (978 07475 6622 9).

C. Choose the best words.

1. ADSL* is more commonly known as _____.
       a. longband   **b.** broadband   **c.** wideband

2. Broadband internet connection is much faster than _____.
       a. dial-in   **b.** dial-through   **c.** dial-up

3. Before you can connect to the internet for the first time, you have to _____ an account with an ISP.
       a. set   **b.** set up   **c.** set in

4. Each time you want to connect to your ISP's system, you have to enter a log-in name and a _____.
       a. security word   **b.** safe word   **c.** password

5. You can set your computer to _____ your log-in details, so you don't have to type them in each time.
       a. store   **b.** remember   **c.** recall

6. With a broadband connection, you usually have to pay a _____.
       a. fixed monthly price   **b.** fixed monthly fee   **c.** fixed monthly cost

7. With dial-up, you can usually choose a _____ tariff.
       a. pay-as-you-go   **b.** pay-what-you-want   **c.** pay-if-you-like

8. Some broadband contracts limit the amount of _____ you can have each month.
       a. pages   **b.** traffic   **c.** use

9. Looking at web pages can be called "navigating the Web" but is more commonly called _____.
       a. "surfing the net"   **b.** "skiing the net"   **c.** "swimming the net"

10. You can often find the answer to a question by _____ on the internet.
       a. looking at it   **b.** looking for it   **c.** looking it up

11. When your computer is not connected to the internet, it is _____.
       a. out of line   **b.** offline   **c.** off the line

12. Internet banking is also called _____.
       a. online banking   **b.** on the line banking   **c.** inline banking

13. An unexpected disconnection from the internet is called a _____.
       a. lost connection   **b.** missed connection   **c.** dropped connection

14. A file which is copied from the internet onto your computer is called _____
       a. an upload   **b.** a download   **c.** a load

15. Downloading files from the internet can _____ your computer with a virus.
       a. infect   **b.** contaminate   **c.** dirty

ADSL stands for asymmetric digital subscriber line, but the full term is almost never used.

For reference see A & C Black *Dictionary of Computing* (978 07475 6622 9).

3.2 Internet browsers

A. Match the browser toolbar button with the function.

1. Back   **a.** Shows a list of the websites you have visited recently.

2. Forward   **b.** Opens the media bar, accessing internet radio, music, video etc.

3. Stop   **c.** Displays the page you were on before.

4. Refresh[1] / Reload[2]   **d.** Shows the latest version of the page.

5. Home   **e.** Opens the search panel.

6. Search   **f.** Displays the page you were on before using the Back button.

7. Favourites[1] / Bookmarks[2]   **g.** Displays the page you have set as your home page.

8. Media   **h.** Prints the current page.

9. History   **i.** Stops a page from downloading.

10. Mail   **j.** Displays the web addresses you have chosen as your favourites

11. Print   **k.** Shows email options.

[1] *Microsoft Internet Explorer;* [2] *Netscape Navigator / Mozilla Firefox*

Quiz

Do you know the answers to these technical questions about browsers? Answer true ***or*** false ***for each one.***

1. All browsers (Internet Explorer, Mozilla Firefox etc) have exactly the same functions.

2. Cookies are data sent by an internet server to a browser. They identify the user, and track the user's access to the server.

3. You can get your browser to delete the cookies it has stored. (In Internet Explorer go to **Tools**, then to **Internet Options**, then to **Delete Cookies**.)

4. Pages you have viewed are stored in the Temporary Internet Files folder. These cannot be deleted.

5. You can tell your browser how long to store web addresses in the History.

6. You can set your browser to block pop-up windows.

7. All pop-ups are advertisements.

8. You can add extra toolbars to your browser window, for example a toolbar from Google.

For reference see A & C Black *Dictionary of Computing* (978 07475 6622 9).

> ### What's the difference between a web directory and a search engine?
>
> Web directories (for example, Excite, Lycos) list categories and sub-categories with links to websites. Search engines (for example, Google, Altavista) search the Web for web pages according to the instructions that you give them.

A. Using a search engine

Put the words into the spaces.

click on	criteria	database	hyperlinks
keywords	matches	media	refine
returns	sponsored	view	

Stage 1: Enter one or more _____.

Stage 2. The search engine looks for _____ in all the web pages on their _____.

Stage 3: The search engine _____ the matches (or "hits") with _____ to the web pages.

Stage 4: The search engine may also return "_____ links". These are links to the websites of companies who have paid the search engine company.

Stage 5: You _____ the hyperlink to _____ the web page.

Stage 6: If necessary, you can _____ your search by using advanced search _____ such as language, country or the type of _____ you are looking for.

B. Logical operators

You can refine your search by using logical operators. Match the search engine instructions with the matches.

1. "English vocabulary"	**a.** Pages where both words appear.
2. English + vocabulary	**b.** Pages containing the phrase *English vocabulary*.
3. English NEAR vocabulary	**c.** Pages containing one of the words, but not both.
4. English OR vocabulary	**d.** Pages where the two words appear close together.
5. English NOT vocabulary	**e.** All pages that contain *English* except the ones which also contain *vocabulary*.

For reference see A & C Black *Dictionary of Computing* (978 07475 6622 9).

3.4 Things on the net

A. Match the activities with the internet features.

1. Keep a public diary of your journey through South America

    a. webmail

2. Lose lots of money

    b. online music store

3. Find out about the First World War

    c. instant messaging

4. Download songs

    d. online radio

5. Listen to music in real time

    e. portal

6. Check your email from any computer

    f. blog

7. Find links to other websites

    g. online encyclopedia

8. Exchange messages in real time with friends or colleagues

    h. currency converter

9. Check the latest exchange rates

    i. e-zine

10. Read new articles about a subject that interests you

    j. online casino

B. Can you match these activities with the internet features? (It's not easy – the terms are sometimes confused with each other.)

Activities	Internet features
1. Exchange messages in real time about anything you like with strangers.	**a.** newsgroup
2. Post messages about your favourite pop group, and maybe reply to other fans' messages.	**b.** forum
3. Exchange information and messages about saving a local wood from development with anybody who wants to join in.	**c.** discussion group
4. Exchange information and views about the economy of Australia with other Australian economists.	**d.** bulletin board / noticeboard
5. Post / download photos, video clips and messages among a group of friends.	**e.** chatroom

For reference see A & C Black *Dictionary of Computing* (978 07475 6622 9).

Choose the best words to complete the sentences.

1. "The website gets a thousand hits a week" means the website has a thousand _____ a week.

    a. sales   **b.** visits   **c.** search engine matches

2. The words, images and other material that make up a website are called _____.

    a. the contents   **b.** the content   **c.** the filling

3. Designs and drawings in websites are usually called _____.

    a. web pictures   **b.** web graphics   **c.** web illustrations

4. Moving pictures in websites are usually called _____.

    a. cartoons   **b.** movies   **c.** animations

5. Websites with sounds and/or video clips and/or animations have _____ content.

    a. multimedia   **b.** many-media   **c.** mixed-media

6. A space in a website where you enter information (address, password etc.) is called a _____.

    a. box   **b.** strip   **c.** field

7. A hyperlink (see 3.3) is often called just _____.

    a. a link   **b.** a hyper   **c.** an HL

8. In real time (see 3.4) means _____.

    a. during working hours **b.** instantly   **c.** in British Standard Time

9. A place with computers for public internet use is usually called an internet café or _____.
even if they don't serve coffee.

    a. web café   **b.** computer café   **c.** cyber café

10. Internet cafés offer internet _____.

    a. connection   **b.** availability   **c.** access

11. A program that adds functions to a browser (eg Shockwave) is called a _____.

    a. plug   **b.** plugged-in   **c.** plug-in

12. Temporary internet files are stored in the _____.

    a. cash   **b.** cache   **c.** cashe

13. Colours which all browsers can display without problems are called _____ colours.

    a. browser safe   **b.** browser acceptable   **c.** browser easy

For reference see A & C Black *Dictionary of Computing* (978 07475 6622 9).

3.6 E-commerce

Shopping on the net

A. Fill the gaps, then put these stages in order (number them 1 to 8).

account   add   browse   checkout

confirm   delivery   details   invoice

shopping basket   sign in

	You usually have to allow at least two working days for 1_____.
	Choose an item, and 2_____ it to your 3_____.
	Click 4 "_____". Now it's too late to change your mind!
	When you have finished shopping, click "proceed to 5_____".
	Usually, you will receive an 6_____ by email
	Enter your name, address and card 7_____.
1	Before you can start shopping, you usually have to 8_____ to the site. (If you don't already have an 9_____, you have to create one.)
	10_____ the website, and decide what you want to buy.

B. Put the words into the spaces.

bid   down   encrypted   online

outbid   padlock   secure server   system

1. Sites that ask for your credit card number or other personal information should use a _____, so the data you send is _____.

2. A: "Have you ever bought anything on an auction site like eBay?"
   B: "No. Once I made a _____ on something, but I was _____ a few seconds before the auction closed."

3. The _____ symbol means that a web-page is secure.

4: I couldn't book my flight _____ because the airline's _____ was _____.

For reference see A & C Black *Dictionary of Computing* (978 07475 6622 9).

Booking a hotel online

C. Choose the best words.

You can often make a hotel reservation [1] **by** /**over** the internet, but you may have to pay a deposit. The deposit will usually be returned [2] **to** / **for** you if you cancel your reservation a week or more [3] **in** / **with** advance.

You will usually receive notification [4] **about** / **of** the booking [5] **by** / **from** email. When you check [6] **in** / **into** the hotel, your details will probably already be [7] **on** / **inside** the hotel system. When you check [8] **out** / **out of**, you will usually be given a receipt.

Filling in an e-form

D. Write the information into the fields.

27/03/1965

213 Wood Street

4044 5055 6066 7077

Anne Mary

amj999@hotmail.com

Apartment 17

Bellevue Apartments

Chicago

Illinois

Jones

Ms

USA

Visa Debit

IL 60611

1 888 999 0000

Name		
Title ___ **Forename(s)** _____		**Surname** _____

Billing address

Line 1	_____
Line 2	_____
Line 3	_____
Town / City	_____
State[1] / Province / County[2]	_____
Zip Code[1] / Postcode[2]	_____
Country	_____
Date of birth	dd/mm/yyyy

Delivery address

If different to billing address, **click here**

Card type	_____
Card number	_____
Daytime telephone number (inc. country code)	+ _____
email address	_____
confirm email address	_____

[1] USA   [2] United Kingdom

E. How is a credit card different to a debit card? Do you have one or both or neither?

For reference see A & C Black *Dictionary of Computing* (978 07475 6622 9).

3. 7 internet security

A. Choose the best words to go into each of the spaces.

1. A person who illegally accesses somebody else's computer over the internet is called a
_____ .
    a. pirate   **b.** hack   **c.** hacker

2. A website which (in theory) cannot be accessed by a hacker is _____ .
    a. strong   **b.** secure   **c.** clean

3. A website which can only be viewed by authorised people has _____ access.
    a. reduced   **b.** small   **c.** restricted

4. Unwanted advertising emails are popularly known as _____ .
    a. meatloaf   **b.** spam   **c.** sausages

5. Software which blocks attempts by others to access your computer over the internet is called a
_____ .
    a. firewall   **b.** fire blanket   **c.** fire engine

6. It's essential to _____ your anti-virus protection regularly.
    a. up-to-date   **b.** date   **c.** update

7. Anti-virus software can _____ your computer for viruses.
    a. detect   **b.** review   **c.** scan

8. Anti-virus software can also _____ viruses on removable media, such as floppy disks.
    a. detect   **b.** control   **c.** see

9. When your anti-virus software subscription _____ ...
    a. ends   **b.** stops   **c.** expires

10. ... it's a good idea to _____ it immediately.
    a. renew   **b.** renovate   **c.** replace

B. Match the malware with the damage. (It's not easy, and the terms are sometimes confused with each other.)

1. **virus**	a. collects and sends private information from the infected computer to a third party
2. **spyware**	b. an undesirable program which can replicate itself across a network
3. **trojan horse**	c. allows a hacker to access private information when he/she wishes
4. **keystroke logger** or **keylogger**	d. a program which adds itself to an executable file, and can cause considerable damage to the data on the infected computer
5. **worm**	e. records characters that are typed into a computer

For reference see A & C Black *Dictionary of Computing* (978 07475 6622 9).

From:	anna@goodmail.com
To:	bernard@ciaociao.it
Cc:	carol@freemail.co.uk
Bcc:	dave@norsemail.no
Subject:	arriving in Rome

Hi Bernard

I'll be arriving in Rome just after midday tomorrow (Friday). You don't need to pick me up at the airport – I can get a taxi to the city centre.

See you soon!

Anna

A. Look at the email and answer the questions true or false.

1. The recipient is Anna.
2. The sender is Anna.
3. Bernard knows that Carol knows when Anna will be arriving in Rome.
4. Bernard knows that Dave knows when Anna will be arriving in Rome.
5. You can say that Anna Cc-ed her email to Carol.
6. You can say that Anna Bcc-ed her email to Dave.
7. The subject line is empty.
8. The style of the email is formal.
9. Cc stands for carbon copy and Bcc stands for blind carbon copy, but the full terms are almost never used.
10. Carbon copies were a method of making copies of documents typed on typewriters.

Sending an attachment

B. Put the words in the spaces.

| attach | browse | field | inboxes |
| open | send | size | |

You can send almost any file as an attachment. [1]_____ through the folders on your computer until you find the file you want to attach. Click on "[2]_____". The file will appear in the attachments [3]_____. Then click "[4]_____", and wait while the file uploads. Add more files if you wish. When you have finished adding files, click "[5]_____".

Some email [6]_____ will only receive attachments up to a certain [7]_____ with one email, for example 10MB. If you need to send a lot of very big attachments, it's sometimes necessary to spread them over a number of separate emails.

For reference see A & C Black *Dictionary of Computing* (978 07475 6622 9).

3.9 Email comprehension 1

Hi Tony

Thanks for sending through that a/w so quickly. Just one problem – I couldn't open the attachment. I'm not sure why. My inbox is virtually empty, so there's plenty of room, and the attachment limit is 20MB, so there's no problem there. Perhaps there was a glitch somewhere. Anyway, rather than trying to figure out what went wrong, could you just send it again?

Did we discuss file format? I don't know much about TIFFs, JPEGs etc, but I meant to tell you that if you have any queries on this, you could get in touch with Steve, our designer. His email address is steve@stevegreendesign.co.uk.

One other thing. When you resend me the a/w, could you cc it to Angela? I've asked her to have a quick look at it before we put it in the brochure.

I'm looking forward very much to seeing those pics – fingers crossed that they'll come through OK this time. However, if I still can't download them, I'll ask you to put them on a disk and mail them.

All the best

Jenny

A. Are these statements *true* or *false*?

1. Jenny didn't receive the a/w because her inbox is too small.
2. The attached files came to less than 20MB in total.
3. Jenny has resolved a technical problem, and the attachment will come through without any problems next time.
4. Tony will have to resend the a/w.
5. Jenny is a graphic design expert
6. Tony is also going to put the files onto a disk and mail them.
7. Angela has already seen the a/w.
8. The style is too informal – business emails should always be more formal than this.

B. Find words or expressions in the email which mean the same as the phrases below.

1. artwork   _____

2. a small technical problem   _____

3. type of file   _____

4. questions about this   _____

5. send again   _____

6. email a copy to   _____

7. communicate with   _____

8. with luck…   _____

For reference see A & C Black *Dictionary of Computing* (978 07475 6622 9).

Dear Jenny

As requested, I'm attaching the a/w files again.

The technical problems you've been experiencing may be due to your email provider. I have to say, I've never heard of Whoopydudu.com. You might be better off switching to one of the big names, such as Gmail or Yahoo.

Regarding file formats, TIFFs should be OK. If necessary, your designer will be able to reformat them very easily, but in my experience most designers have no problem working with TIFFs.

As the file sizes are quite large, and I understand that Angela only has a dial-up connection, I've sent her low-res versions to look at. I hope that will be OK. They should be clear enough.

I'm just about to go on holiday, so if you need me to send these files on disk, please let me know by Friday afternoon. I probably won't get the opportunity to check my email while I'm away, but if anything arises that won't keep, my assistant Trevor may be able to deal with it.

Best regards

Tony

A. Are these statements *true* or *false*?

1. Tony thinks Jenny should change her email provider.

2. The designer will need to reformat the files.

3. Angela doesn't have broadband.

4. Tony is sending resized versions of the a/w files to Angela.

5. These versions will look the same as the original versions.

6. Tony is going on holiday on Friday morning.

7. Trevor may be able to help with any problems that come up while Tony is away.

8. The style is neutral – neither formal nor informal.

B. Find words or expressions in the email which mean the same as the phrases below.

1. as you asked   _____

2. famous companies   _____

3. change the type of file   _____

4. I think, but I may be wrong…   _____

5. Low image resolution (see 1.6)   _____

6. on Friday afternoon or before   _____

7. comes up   _____

8. that's urgent   _____

For reference see A & C Black *Dictionary of Computing* (978 07475 6622 9).

3.11 Useful verbs crossword

Complete the sentences with the missing verbs, and write them into the crossword puzzle. Words in brackets mean the same as the missing verbs.

1. _____ your holiday photos on the web *(display)*

2. _____ the attachment in a new window

3. _____ pop-ups *(stop)*

4. _____ to the internet

5 →. _____ your wireless connection *(turn on)*

5 ↓. _____ your credit card details *(type in)*

6. _____ your anti-virus protection

7. _____ the photo as a JPEG

8. _____ a technical problem *(sort out)*

9. _____ on your firewall *(enable)*

10. _____ your wireless connection *(turn off)*

11. _____ your webpage to a web server

12. _____ some clipart from the internet

13. _____ an attachment with an email

14. _____ for something on eBay

15 →. _____ pop-ups *(permit)*

15. ↓ _____ the internet *(use)*

16. _____ the email to everybody else on the team *(send a copy of)*

17. _____ a bid for something on eBay

18. _____ to a different ISP *(change)*

For reference see A & C Black *Dictionary of Computing* (978 07475 6622 9).

There are 33 words connected with internet in this grid. Can you find them all? (Look down and across.)

```
b  q  q  t  s  y  z  b  x  d  o  m  a  i  n  y  k  n  l  p
r  v  i  r  u  s  u  l  i  i  z  x  s  e  c  u  r  e  o  h
o  a  r  s  r  p  o  o  c  s  a  t  x  e  r  t  y  w  i  y
w  t  e  d  f  h  w  g  l  c  s  o  c  m  c  j  y  s  u  p
s  d  f  b  g  f  j  g  k  o  s  o  v  a  h  k  t  g  f  e
e  n  c  r  y  p  t  i  o  n  e  l  j  i  a  h  u  r  i  r
r  s  a  o  v  b  v  g  b  n  h  b  b  l  t  i  r  o  r  l
z  c  x  a  n  h  a  c  k  e  r  a  u  p  r  o  l  u  e  i
m  u  p  d  a  t  e  x  c  c  b  r  n  n  o  m  e  p  w  n
u  f  d  b  s  a  z  h  i  t  s  n  n  b  o  w  q  q  a  k
l  g  p  a  s  s  w  o  r  d  v  w  e  b  m  a  i  l  l  d
t  h  j  n  e  w  q  f  b  v  c  c  x  z  a  s  h  g  l  f
i  c  l  d  r  u  i  f  n  s  p  y  w  a  r  e  j  k  l  p
m  o  p  o  t  y  q  l  m  l  o  i  o  p  a  d  l  o  c  k
e  o  i  n  b  o  x  i  b  n  r  m  w  i  e  w  e  r  u  y
d  k  q  r  w  x  c  n  v  a  t  t  a  c  h  m  e  n  t  q
i  i  y  t  e  z  r  e  l  o  a  d  b  i  o  r  p  h  k  l
a  e  i  u  a  g  f  d  s  n  l  u  w  e  b  s  i  t  e  j
p  s  o  k  e  y  w  o  r  d  x  y  c  v  t  f  e  w  g  q
j  l  s  p  a  m  h  h  m  z  a  s  s  d  l  a  u  n  c  h
```

email _____   _____   _____

_____   _____   _____

_____   _____   _____

_____   _____   _____

_____   _____   _____

_____   _____   _____

_____   _____   _____

_____   _____   _____

_____   _____   _____

For reference see A & C Black *Dictionary of Computing* (978 07475 6622 9).

3.13 Your internet

1. Who is your current ISP?

_____

2. Have you had any problems with them? If so, what?

_____

3. What type of internet connection do you have?

_____

4. Is it fast enough for your requirements? If not, how would a faster connection be useful to you?

_____

5. From where do you usually access the internet?

_____

6. On average, how many hours a week do you spend online?

_____

7. Have you ever done these things?
   a. sent and received emails
   b. chatted in real time
   c. booked a flight online
   d. used your credit or debit card to pay for something over the internet
   e. had a virus on your computer
   f. had a problem with identity theft
   g. downloaded a photo from a bulletin board
   h. connected to the internet over a wireless connection
   i. set up a wireless network in your own home or office

For reference see A & C Black *Dictionary of Computing* (978 07475 6622 9).

1.1 Hardware

From left to right:

> laptop computer / desktop computer
>
> mouse / printer / scanner
>
> digital camera / fax machine / mobile phone
>
> PDA / projector
>
> docking station / battery / cable / socket / plug

1.2 Some useful verbs

1 f, 2 e, 3 c, 4 d, 5 g, 6 h, 7 b, 8 a, 9 b, 10 c, 11 a, 12 a, 13 b, 14 c, 15 b, 16 b, 17 a, 18 c

1.3 The workstation

1 tower, 2 power button, 3 floppy disk drive, 4 CD / DVD drive, 5 screen, 6 wire / cable, 7 keyboard, 8 mouse, 9 key, 10 flat panel monitor, 11 CRT (Cathode Ray Tube) monitor, 12, stand, 13 printer, 14 scanner, 15 desk, 16 chair, 17 telephone, 18 a, 19 c, 20 a, 21 b, 22 b, 23 c, 24 c, 25 b, 26 a, 27 c.

1.4 The keyboard

Part 1: (clockwise from top left) function keys / indicator lights / calculator keys / return key / alphabet keys / space bar

Part 2: 1 backspace key, 2 shift key, 3 caps lock key, 4 tab key, 5 control key, 6 alt key, 7 escape key, 8 delete key, 9 enter, 10, key in, 11 data input, 12 standard keyboard / ergonomic keyboard

1.5 The mouse

1 scroll up, 2 scroll down, 3 hold down, 4 repetitive strain injury, 5 touchpad (or mouse pad), 6 joystick, 7 roll, 8 optical, 9 single, 10 double, 11 on, 12 left button, 13 right button, 14 scroll wheel (or mouse wheel), 15 pointer

1.6 Scanning

1 connected, 2 original, 3 at / dpi, 4 preview, 5 adjust / brightness / contrast, 6 click, 7 text / OCR software, 8 file format, 9 image editing software, 10 all-in-one, 11 handheld, 12 flatbed, 13 high, 14 low

1.7 Some useful adjectives

1 b, 2 b, 3 c, 4 a, 5 c, 6 a, 7 c, 8 c, 9 a, 10 c, 11 b, 12 a, 13 a, 14 c, 15 c, 16 b

For reference see A & C Black *Dictionary of Computing* (978 07475 6622 9).

1.8 Printing

A: 1 cartridge, 2 replacement, 3 cover, 4 via, 5 out of / reload, 6 jammed, 7 feed, 8 out, 9 mono, 10 print-heads (or print nozzles), 11 double-sided (or two-sided), 12 collate, 13 portrait, 14 landscape

B: 2 laser, 3 laser, 4 laser, 5 inkjet, 6 laser, 7 laser, 8 inkjet

C: 1 T, 2 F (the colours are cyan, magenta, yellow and black), 3 T, 4 F (they're much slower than that), 5 F, 6 T, 7 F, 8 T, 9 T, 10 F

1.9 Mobile phones

Part 1: (from the top) earpiece / screen / keypad / star key / hash key / microphone

Part 2: 1 networks, 2 operators, 3 tariffs, 4 pay-as-you-go, 5 top up, 6 users, 7 contract, 8 SIM card, 9 installed, 10 roaming.

Part 3: 1 b, 2 a, 3 a, 4 b, 5 c, 6 b, 7 a, 8 a, 9 c, 10 c, 11 b, 12 c, 13 d, 14 d, 15 b

1.10 Other devices

1 h, 2 a, 3 g, 4 h, 5 d, 6 c, 7 e, 8 f, 9 b, 10 a, 11 b, 12 b, 13 c, 14 c, 15 b

1.11 Inside a computer

A: 1 processor, 2 chips, 3 dual core, 4 speed, 5 megahertz, 6 megabytes, 7 motherboard, 8 upgraded

B: 1 mains electricity, 2 transformer, 3 surge protector / spikes, 4 disconnect / supply / shock, 5 fan / overheating

1.12 Data storage

Part 1: 1 hard drive, 2 free space, 3 capacity, 4 burn, 5 eject, 6 drawer, 7 card / stick

Part 2: 2 e, 3 c, 4 d, 5 a, 6 g, 7 f

1.13 Connectivity

Part 1: 1 b, 2 a, 3 c, 4 b, 5 c, 6 a, 7 c, 8 b, 9 a

Part 2: 1 wireless, 2 devices, 3 enabled, 4 signals, 5 data, 6 developed, 7 telecommunications

1.14 Networks

LAN: 1 Local, 2 server, 3 terminals, 4 log onto, 5 intranet, 6 satellite, 7 WAN, 8 network card

Network topologies: 1 star, 2 hierarchical, 3 ring, 4 line or bus

1.15 Electronic payments

A: cash / outlets / central / goods / touch / receipts / funds / debit

B: 1 f, 2 c, 3 b, 4 h, 5 a, 6 d, 7 e, 8 g

C: 1 b, 2 a, 3 e, 4 d, 5 c

For reference see A & C Black *Dictionary of Computing* (978 07475 6622 9).

1.16 Review crossword

2.1 Software: the basics

A: 1 b, 2 a, 3 a, 4 c, 5 c, 6 a, 7 b, 8 a, 9 c, 10 b, 11 b, 12 a, 13 b, 14 c

B: 1 installed, 2 launch, 3 renamed, 4 running / close, 5 start menu, 6 window, 7 drag and drop, 8 search / find, 9 user / password, 10 free up / uninstalling, 11 save

2.2 Using software: useful verbs

Set 1: 1 f, 2 e, 3 d, 4 b, 5 c, 6 a

Set 2: 1 d, 2 f, 3 b, 4 a, 5e, 6 c

Set 3: 1 b, 2 c, 3 e, 4 a, 5 f, 6 d

Set 4: 1 c, 2 a, 3 b, 4 e, 5 f, 6 d

2.3 The control panel

2 adding, 3 setting up, 4 format, 5 displayed, 6 background, 7 digital, 8 wallpaper, 9 image, 10 screen saver, 11 wireless, 12 performance, 13 properties, 14 tasks, 15 default

For reference see A & C Black *Dictionary of Computing* (978 07475 6622 9).

2.4 Applications

A: 1 c, 2 d, 3 f, 4 b, 5 a, 6 i, 7 g, 8 e, 9 h

B:

NOTES

A security code (no. 8) can also be called *a product registration code* or *product licence code*.

A bootleg (no. 10) can also be called a *pirate copy*.

2.5 Some useful adjectives

A: 1 b, 2 a, 3 a, 4 c, 5 a, 6 c, 7 a, 8 b, 9 c

B: 1 e, 2 d, 3 b, 4 a, 5 c

2.6 Word processing 1

A:

2	top margin
11	bottom margin
1	left-hand margin
12	right-hand margin
3	heading (or title)
5	body text
6	paragraph break
7	indent
8	illustration
9	illustration border (or frame)
10	page number
4	page border (or edge of the page)

B: 1 upper case (or capital letters), 2 lower case (or small letters), 3 plain text, 4 bold, 5 italic, 6 bold italic, 7 underline, 8 strikethrough, 9 outline, 12 shadow

C: 1 b, 2 c, 3 b, 4 a, 5 b, 6 a

For reference see A & C Black *Dictionary of Computing* (978 07475 6622 9).

2.7 Word processing 2

A: 1 b, 2 a, 3 a, 4 c, 5 b, 6 b, 7 a

B: 1 e, 2 c, 3 a, 4 m, 5 g, 6 j, 7 p, 8 s, 9 d, 10 i, 11 u, 12 o, 13 t, 14 r, 15 k, 16 l, 17 w, 18 f, 19 v, 20 x, 21 b, 22 n, 23 q, 24 h

C: 1 true, 2 false (three columns and four rows), 3 true (also known as "white on black" or "WoB"), 4 false (it's the other way round), 5 true, 6 false (they're black).

2.8 Word processing 3

A: 1 b, 2 d, 3 e, 4 h, 5 c, 6 j, 7 i, 8 f, 9 a, 10 g

B: 1 e, 2 a, 3 c, 4 f, 5 g, 6 h, 7 d, 8 b

C: 1 false (it's been rotated 90 degrees anti-clockwise), 2 false, 3 true, 4 true

D: 1 c, 2 c, 3 b, 4 a, 5 a, 6 c, 7 a, 8 c, 9 b, 10 a

2.9 Image editing

A: 1 d, 2 i, 3 j, 4 f, 5 g, 6 b, 7 a, 8 c, 9 e, 10 h

B: 1 false, 2 true, 3 true, 4 false (the word is **thumbnails**), 5 true

2.10 Graphic design

1 import, 2 export, 3 frame, 4 gradient, 5 kerning, 6 object, 7 layers, 8 overlaps, 9 blurred, 10, effect, 11 feathering, 12 full bleed, 13 slug, 14 stretched, 15 to press, 16 proofs, 17 presses, 18 separation, 19 plates, 20 converted, 21 reprographics

2.11 Spreadsheets

A: 1 a, 2 c, 3 c, 4 b, 5 c, 6 b, 7 a, 8 c, 9 c, 10 c, 11 b, 12 a

B:

symbol	verb	noun	everyday speech
+	add	addition	"five plus three equals eight"
-	subtract	subtraction	"five minus three equals two"
*	multiply	multiplication	"five multiplied by three equals fifteen" "five times three equals fifteen"
/	divide	division	"fifteen divided by three equals five"
^	raise to the power of		"ten to the power of five is 100,000"

C: 1 true, 2 false (descending), 3 false (ascending), 4 true

D: 1 text, 2 values, 3 boxes, 4 series, 5 appearance

For reference see A & C Black *Dictionary of Computing* (978 07475 6622 9).

2.12 Presentation software
1 b, 2 a, 3 c, 4 c, 5 c, 6 a, 7 a, 8 b, 9 a, 10 c

2.13 Problems with software
Prepositions: 1 on / of, 3 to, 5 in, 6 on, 7 in, 8 to, 9 on, a from, d on, e down, g with, h to / on
Matching: 1 b, 2 g, 3 e, 4 f, 5 d, 6 h, 7 i, 8 c, 9 a

2.14 Which program?
(Features generally associated with application types – some versions may have different features.)

	word processor	spreadsheet	image editor	media player
1. select text	x	x		
2. save as JPEG			x	
3. insert table	x			
4. play				x
5. touch up			x	
6. import photo	x		x	
7. exit	x	x	x	x
8. copy from CD				x
9. check internet for updates	x	x	x	x
10. copy block of cells	x	x		
11. insert text box	x			
12. page set-up	x	x		
13. optimise for internet			x	
14. uninstall	x	x	x	x
15. add border	x	x		
16. insert bullet points	x			
17. convert to MP3				x
18. paste into new document	x	x		
19. check spelling	x	x		
20. change text direction	x			
21. flip, crop and rotate			x	
22. sort	x	x		
23. alter formula values		x		
24. create playlist				x
25. print	x	x	x	
26. clear all cells		x		
27. maximise window	x	x	x	x
28. insert column break	x			
29. convert to greyscale			x	
30. open	x	x	x	x

2.15 Revision quiz
1. Windows (95/98/2000/ME/XP), Mac (OS9, OSX etc), Linux, 2. The recycle bin, 3. Wallpaper, 4. The control panel, 5. An image editor, 6. A media player, 7. Freeware, 8. Capital letters in highlighted bold italic underline, 9. Arial 9 point double spaced, 10. A template, 11. The clipboard, 12. It's a mirror image of the original, 13. Softening an image, 14. Thumbnails, 15. To sort, 16. A cell, 17 A slideshow, 18. A bug, 19. It compresses files, 20. Drivers, 21. Columns and rows, 22. Dollar sign, 23. ampersand, 24. asterisk (or multiply sign), 25. hash, 26. brackets, 27. forward slash (or divide sign), 28. backward slash, 29. question mark, 30. plus sign

For reference see A & C Black *Dictionary of Computing* (978 07475 6622 9).

3.1 The internet: the basics

A: 1 network, 2 over, 3 servers, 4 access, 5 provider, 6 discussion

B:

6/7	close down your browser
1/2	connect to your ISP
6/7	disconnect from the internet
3	enter a web address (also known as a URL)
1/2	launch your browser (for example, Internet Explorer, Netscape Navigator or Mozilla Firefox)
4	perhaps wait for a few seconds while the web-page downloads
5	view the page

C: 1 b, 2 c, 3 b, 4 c, 5 b, 6 b, 7 a, 8 b, 9 a, 10 c, 11 b, 12 a, 13 c, 14 b, 15 a

3.2 Internet browsers

A: 1 c, 2 f, 3 i, 4 d, 5 g, 6 e, 7 j, 8 b, 9 a, 10 k, 11 h

B:

1. False. They are similar, but there are some minor differences.

2. True

3. True

4. False – they can be deleted (in Internet Explorer, go to **Tools / Internet Options / Delete Files**)

5. True

6. True

7. False. Many are advertisements, but information about program updates etc. is also sometimes displayed as pop-ups.

8. True

3.3 Search engines

A: 1 keywords, 2 matches / database, 3 returns / hyperlinks, 4 sponsored, 5 click on / view, 6 refine / criteria / media

B: 1 b, 2 a, 3 d, 4 c, 5 e

3.4 Things on the net

A: 1 f, 2 j, 3 g, 4 b, 5 d, 6 a, 7 e, 8 c, 9 h, 10 i

B: 1 e, 2 c, 3 a, 4 b, 5 d *(but note that a, b and c are sometimes confused with each other)*

3.5 Internet terms

1 b, 2 b, 3 b, 4 c, 5 a, 6 c, 7 a, 8 b, 9 c, 10 c, 11c, 12 b, 13 a

For reference see A & C Black *Dictionary of Computing* (978 07475 6622 9).

3.6 E-commerce

A:

8	You usually have to allow at least two working days for [1] <u>delivery</u>.
3	Choose an item, and [2] <u>add</u> it to your [3] <u>shopping basket</u>.
6	Click [4] "<u>confirm</u>". Now it's too late to change your mind!
4	When you have finished shopping, click "proceed to [5] <u>checkout</u>".
7	Usually, you will receive an [6] <u>invoice</u> by email.
5	Enter your name, address and card [7] <u>details</u>.
1	Before you can start shopping, you usually have to [8] <u>sign in</u> to the site. (If you don't already have an [9] <u>account</u>, you have to create one.)
2	[10] <u>Browse</u> the website, and decide what you want to buy.

B: 1 secure server / encrypted, 2 bid / outbid, 3 padlock, 4 online / system / down

C: 1 over, 2 to, 3 in, 4 of, 5 by, 6 into, 7 on, 8 out

D:
Name
  Title: Ms
  Forename(s): Anne Mary
  Surname: Jones
Billing address
  Line 1: Apartment 17
  Line 2: Bellevue Apartments
  Line 3: 213 Wood Street
  Town / City: Chicago
  State[1] / Province / County[2]: Illinois
  Zip Code[1] / Postcode[2]: IL 60611
  Country: USA
Date of birth: 27/03/1965
Card type: Visa debit
Card number: 4044 5055 6066 7077
Daytime telephone number (inc. country code) +1 888 999 0000
email address: amj999@hotmail.com
confirm email address: amj999@hotmail.com

E: When you pay by debit card, the money is taken almost immediately from your bank account. When you pay by credit card, you don't have to pay anything until you receive a bill from the credit card company.

3.7 Internet security
A: 1 c, 2 b, 3 c, 4 b, 5 a, 6 c, 7 c, 8 a, 9 c, 10 a

B: 1 d, 2 a, 3 c, 4 e, 5 b

For reference see A & C Black *Dictionary of Computing* (978 07475 6622 9).

3.8 Email

A: 1 false (the recipient is Bernard), 2 true, 3 true, 4 false, 5 true, 6 true, 7 false, 8 false, 9 true, 10, true

B: 1 browse, 2 open, 3 field, 4 attach, 5 send, 6 inboxes, 7 size

3.9 Email comprehension 1

A: 1 false, 2 true, 3 false, 4 true, 5 false, 6 false, 7 false, 8 false – some business emails are very informal, other are very formal. It depends on the situation.

B: 1 a/w, 2 glitch (informal word), 3 file format, 4 queries on this, 5 resend, 6 cc, 7 get in touch with, 8 fingers crossed

3.10 Email comprehension 2

A: 1 true, 2 false, 3 true, 4 true, 5 false, 6 false, 7 true, 8 true. Some of the language is quite informal, but the email begins and ends with Dear… and Best regards, and the tone is not particularly friendly.

B: as requested, 2 big names, 3 reformat, 4 I understand that…, 5 low-res, 6 by Friday afternoon, 7 arises, 8 that won't keep

3.11 Useful verbs crossword

1 post
2 open
3 block
4 connect
5 across – enable, 5 down – enter
6 update
7 reformat
8 resolve
9 turn (on)
10 disable
11 upload
12 download
13 send
14 bid
15 across – allow, 15 down – access
16 cc (used as a verb)
17 make
18 switch

For reference see A & C Black *Dictionary of Computing* (978 07475 6622 9).

Answer key (cont.)

3.12 Revision wordsearch

```
b       s     b   d o m a i n       n
r v i r u s   l   i     s e c u r e     h
o     r     o   s   t   e         w   y
w     f     g   c   o   m c       s   p
s   b         o   o   a h       g f e
e n c r y p t i o n   l   i   a   r i r
r   o           n   b   l   t   o r l
    a   h a c k e r a       r   u e i
m u p d a t e     c   r       o   p w n
u   b       h i t s       o       a k
l   p a s s w o r d     w   b m a i l l
t   n                         l
i c   d       s p y w a r e
m o           o     p a d l o c k
e o i n b o x     r
d k           a t t a c h m e n t
i i       r e l o a d
a e           l   w e b s i t e
  s   k e y w o r d
  s p a m           l a u n c h
```

email	hacker	portal
attachment	hits	reload
blog	hyperlink	secure
broadband	inbox	spam
browser	keyword	spyware
chatroom	launch	surf
cookies	multimedia	toolbar
disconnect	newsgroup	update
domain	offline	virus
encryption	padlock	webmail
firewall	password	website

For reference see A & C Black *Dictionary of Computing* (978 07475 6622 9).

References refer to the unit number

For reference see A & C Black *Dictionary of Computing* (978 07475 6622 9).

For reference see A & C Black *Dictionary of Computing* (978 07475 6622 9).

For reference see A & C Black *Dictionary of Computing* (978 07475 6622 9).

For reference see A & C Black *Dictionary of Computing* (978 07475 6622 9).

For reference see A & C Black *Dictionary of Computing* (978 07475 6622 9).

Acknowledgements

Adobe®, PageMaker®, Photoshop®and InDesign® are trademarks of Adobe Systems Inc.

Microsoft®, Windows® and PowerPoint® are trademarks of the Microsoft corporation.

Mozilla Firefox™ is a trademark of the Mozilla Foundation.

Netscape® is a trademark of Netscape Communication Corps.

Norton AntiVirus® is a trademark of Symantec Corporation.

RealPlayer™ is a trademark of RealNetworks Inc.

WinZip™ is a registered trademark of WinZip Computing Inc.

For reference see A & C Black *Dictionary of Computing* (978 07475 6622 9).